96 WAYS TO RISE AND GRIND

C.D. CARTER

authorHOUSE®

AuthorHouse™
1663 Liberty Drive
Bloomington, IN 47403
www.authorhouse.com
Phone: 1 (800) 839-8640

Published by AuthorHouse 03/13/2017

ISBN: 978-1-5246-5493-1 (sc)
ISBN: 978-1-5246-5491-7 (hc)
ISBN: 978-1-5246-5492-4 (e)

Library of Congress Control Number: 2016920721

Print information available on the last page.

Any people depicted in stock imagery provided by Thinkstock are models, and such images are being used for illustrative purposes only. Certain stock imagery © Thinkstock.

Th is book is printed on acid-free paper.

FOREWORD

Everyone with an internet connection, it seems, is rising and grinding. And somewhere in between the rising and the grinding, these risers and grinders find time to tell the world that they are, in fact, rising and grinding. They use the hashtag #RiseAndGrind as a clarion call not just to those fellow risers and grinders grinding away out there in the world, but to those who are not rising and/or grinding.

For one to rise and shine seems quaint in this Age of Rising and Grinding on various social media outlets brimming with the rising and grinding hoards attached at the eyeballs to their Twitter and Facebook and Instagram accounts. We must grind, then publicize the grind. I've tweeted for a couple years about this pervasive rising and grinding, having a little fun along the way at the expense of the droves of devoted risers and grinders. This book is filled with many of the satirical missives that, hopefully, make a point about the culture of rising and grinding while bringing a smile to the faces of those who might roll their eyes at always-earnest rise-and-grind tweets.

The rising part of the two-step process has remained the same, for one must rise before one does anything. It's noteworthy – disconcerting, I'd argue – that the latter step has changed, morphing into something implying drudgery, some sort of undesirable, irrepressible, desperate effort. No longer do we shine when we awake – arms stretched overhead, brains slowly coming into focus for a new day. Now we grind. We work, we sweat, we strive, we move, we push, we do, we will ourselves: we grind.

Drudgery has become sport in this grind-centric culture – a badge of honor we wear with puffed chests. We brag about working long, exhausting hours. We take pride in our lack of sleep, our refusal to listen to our bodies and rest. We don't dare imply that we have time to relax, to do nothing, to offset the effects of the grind. We must, at all costs, convince people that we grind and grind and grind because there's dignity in grinding.

What were we created to do if not grind? God made grinders, and they were good.

The wholesale replacement of shining with grinding is equal parts telling, inevitable, and, in my considered estimation, worrisome. Rise and shine surely means different things to different people, but to me the phrase implies something overtly and unashamedly positive, something cheery and uplifting. My mom, when she woke me up for school from my dead adolescent sleep, would declare that it was time to rise and shine. She would rub my back with the sort of tenderness that can't be mimicked. I still – as a 30-something married father of two – miss that wonderful awakening. I guess I always will.

There's a carefree element to rising and shining. To rise and shine is to simply be – not to force anything, not to make anything happen. Rise and be yourself. Rise and do what needs to be done, but also do what you would like to do. If you're alive in a developed, post-industrial society, you likely have to do some amount of grinding to maintain a roof over your head and food in your belly. Grinding undoubtedly has its place: to ensure your survival. But it's only one of those two – shining, not grinding – that brings to mind my son's Sesame Street books, full of idyllic scenes in which people (and furry monsters) work, but also do what they want to do, what conjures joy. They paint and sing, they play games and dance, they laugh and talk about nothing of import. In short, they shine.

Shining – to give forth or glow with light – has a communal element. You're not shining just for you, but for those around you – family, friends, and strangers alike. Something that shines is radiant and bright. It reaches out beyond itself.

To shine is to obliterate darkness. I'm a cynical person, so I have no illusions that darkness can be repelled forever. It can't. Whether you think darkness is the end of your existence or simply a transition to some other level of existence is up to you. Shining, it seems, is the way to hold back that darkness, if just for a bit. Life is a short, warm moment, as Pink Floyd said. Shining makes it so.

Rising and shining has an undeniably utopian element, whereas rising and grinding – its grittier, stone-faced, fun-shunning cousin – has a most definite post-apocalyptic feel. You know who rises and grinds? Characters in the Mad Max movies. They grind in abject misery, in a world of libertarian fantasies, where civil society has been summarily replaced by a brutal hellscape in which everyone fends of themselves and no one else.

That, in summary, is grinding.

I don't think it's a coincidence that that phrase – that dictate – has come to prominence in the age of crushing economic austerity, roiling, hopelessly corrupt international markets racked by bowel-shaking greed and fear, and an entire generation of political leaders that has never once questioned the underpinnings of unfettered self interest. What's good for you is good for you. Get yours. Do you. If your neighbor didn't get hers, she didn't deserve it. Plain and simple.

Grind on and be free: the phrase almost oozes from the American ethos. If everyone were a dedicated riser and grinder, we hear, everything would be okay.

There's an innate selfishness in rising and grinding. There's an implication that you are all that matters, that there is no vast universe, but only your needs and desires. Grind to eat, grind to purchase, grind to upgrade, grind to get more and more and more, grind because someone somewhere is grinding harder than you. Grind because you're afraid. Look over your shoulder and grind. Fear and grind. Feel pangs of terror in your heart and grind.

No one ever shined their way to the top, we're told. They grind to the top, like a possessed upside down drill spinning recklessly through the floors of a skyscraper, destroying everyone and everything in its path without a modicum of remorse because there are no victims in the World of Grinding. There are only volunteers.

Humankind competes today for diminishing resources. That goes for everyday working people more than any other group. Wages have stagnated and oceans of money sit above our heads, out of reach, protected by elites and safe from taxation. We've been left to fight in the Thunderdome for the scraps – the crumbs – falling from the tables of our moneyed masters. So we grind. We grind over and through each other. We grind in offices, hoping and praying that our grinding will one day – someday – pay off. We are pitted against each other in a daily grinding match. There's no time to even question why we're grinding, or who benefits when we grind against fellow workers. We become machines programmed to do one thing: grind.

Who benefits from your endless grinding? Who cares? Just grind. And when you're done grinding, grind some more.

The deafening drumbeat of the daily grind has only recently taken on the form of tweets, but the message that drives our collective grind has been with us for a long while. And it's worked for those at the top of the grinding food chain. A steady rise in worker productivity was met with an almost identical increase in worker wages from 1948-1973, but a 73.4 percent spike in American workers' net productivity from 1973-2015 coincided with near-total wage stagnation, according to a study from the Economic Policy Institute (EPI). This means, in short, that Americans are working harder than ever, producing more than ever, with nothing to show for it. If wages had grown as productivity jumped, an American worker with an annual income of $50,000 today would make upwards of $75,000 per year, according to EPI research.

We're not reaping the fruits of our daily grind. It's the beneficiaries of your grind – your labor – who don't want you to know these ugly little economic facts, or to ask who has, in fact, reaped the fruits of your labor. Yet we have billionaires fighting any and all efforts for fast food workers to earn a livable wage. Business magnates have set out to dismantle labor unions to ensure that collective grinding – and bargaining – is made toothless. People who own more homes than you own pairs of pants refuse to let you share the benefits of a 42-year increase in productivity. They rise and know you'll grind.

Our eternal grind is at least partly based on our cultural obsession with chasing happiness. An entire industry has developed around our desire to be happy, to be content, to do whatever it takes to achieve some level of serenity. Books, DVDs, and all manner of media appeal to our wrenching desperation to be happy. Tweets about the ways in which people rise and grind indicate – if not outright declare – that grinding is the path to happiness. Much of the rise-and-grind subtext charges that grinding is, in fact, the key to happiness.

The opposite is true.

A Stanford University study that drew data from more than 500,000 people, tracking "day-to-day fluctuations and patterns in people's emotions," found that people's feelings of well being were lowest during the workweek. Those good feelings – that happiness – peaked on the weekends. These findings might not stun you. What proved surprising, however, was that the pattern was the same for unemployed people who responded to the survey. Their stress and anxiety were highest during the workweek, just like their counterparts who were sitting in cubicle farms, sweating under a hardhat, or hustling out food and drinks for ungrateful customers.

But there we have it, in indisputable, cold, hard numbers: happiness levels spike on the weekends both for people who work and those who don't.

That's because, according to researchers, the weekend doesn't just serve as a respite from the horrors of the workweek grind. The weekend gives us what truly brings happiness: time together with friends and family. Grinding or no grinding, being together with those we love is when key happiness indicators go through the proverbial roof. Grinding away at the job that we may or may not hate might offer a path to some semblance of a happy life, but grinding in and of itself – according to half a million people – is not the happiness skeleton key.

It's hardly an overstatement to say that we're happiest when we're freed from the clutches of the grind, if only for forty-eight fleeting weekend hours.

There's more than a kernel of isolationist thinking in rising and grinding. Read the avalanche of tweets trumpeting various versions of rising and grinding and you'll quickly see that grinding is done by oneself, for oneself. There are certainly people grinding (working) every day for their partners and kids and family members, but the phenomenon is, in many ways, a uniquely American one: we are cowboys, alone in the expanse, independent of everyone and everything, alienated from everyone and everything, cast out into the world to get what we can get.

There is no such thing as rising and grinding as a team of people with a common cause. There is no longer a collective grinding – a massive sigh of relief for those at the top who know, deep in their marrow, that collective grinding would be the demise of the gravy train they believe will never end.

Social science has shown that human beings value fairness highly, and that we're not innately selfish creatures who prefer to exist alone, separated from the tribe. The system in which we exist preaches individualism over everything. Selfishness is the ultimate virtue. We live in Ayn Rand's dream world: one of laissez faire capitalism for the middle and working classes, and of comfortable socialism for the upper echelon. They have their vampire fangs sunk deep into our flesh. Those fangs have been there so long, jammed into us, that we hardly notice anymore. We don't fight the bite. We instead buy into the worldview of the people and institutions that put those fangs there. We learn to love our sharp-toothed parasites. We've decided, as a people, that grinding is our best option. Perhaps it's our only option.

Rise and cede to the hypnotism of our masters and grind.

Does grinding have its place? I don't think there's a question that yes, it does. The single mother of two grinds like hell so her children won't starve. The married couple grinds so they can take care of a sick mother whose body no longer allows for grinding. The college kid from the slums grinds to make the most of his scholarship, or his parents' hard-earned cash. The high school athlete grinds past the limits of exhaustion because she loves the game – it makes her happy.

Grinding surely has a place in the world.

But rising and grinding as a credo – as a slogan for how you live out the oh-so-finite days of your life – is a myopic approach that doesn't just limit the shine in your life. Unquestioned devotion to grinding snuffs out the shine. Grinding culture says people are expendable, human connection is meaningless and that, at heart, everyone is a killer.

I reject that.

No part of me doubts that everyone has a desire to shine somewhere underneath the persona they've created, the one presented to the world every day, with varying degrees of honesty. Any person who has been compelled to perform a mindless task in exchange for a little money must eventually ask the question: Is this what I was put here to do?

What a terrifyingly important question.

To question the purpose of your existence is inconvenient, uncomfortable, gut wrenching, and critically important. Without pondering that question, what are we but talking monkeys with checking accounts? And to shine, in my estimation, is to do that which offers a satisfactory answer to that all-important question.

For some, shining might be creating: writing, drawing, painting, filming, molding, building. For others it might be working in nature, ending the day with dirt caked beneath fingernails, drenched in sweat from the unrelenting heat of the sun, admiring things and creatures that neither grind nor shine, but just are. Shining might be helping those caught in the merciless undertow of grinding culture, folks who need a helping hand, a bite to eat or a place to stay. Shining for some might be as simple and common as reading a book that changes the way you see a sliver of your world, or watching a movie that forces you to feel something long hidden – to confront something buried. Rising and shining can be a revolutionary act.

Shining is happiness, both giving it and receiving it. Grinding and happiness are not mutually exclusive, but that grind is not centered on the answer to that infernal question: Is this what I was put here to do?

Maybe, just maybe, the directions to shining over grinding lie in a classic lyric from a classic song: "Remember when you were young," begins Pink Floyd's "Shine on You Crazy Diamond." "You shone like the sun."

You rose and shined as a kid. I did too. We all did. Make like the you from so long ago and don't grind. Shine.

DEDICATION

To Melissa, whose love shines, and always has. To Xavier and Eleanor, may the brightness of your smiles obliterate the darkness in this world.

Rise

with a thousand ambassadors of
the morning sun on your eyelids

tell them to go the hell back home

and grind.

Rise and pretend your cereal is healthy

and stare, horrified, at the nutrition facts

eat it anyway

and grind.

Rise

and see that the grey hairs in your
beard are a fast-growing minority

ready to take over

consider your own
decay and grind.

Rise and make some coffee

and warm up said coffee in the microwave

and forget the coffee is in the microwave

and grind.

Rise

and change all your fantasy
football lineups

and question your life choices

and grind.

Rise and resent all the
time you spend

watching terrible TV shows

and wonder how smart you'd be if
you read more

and grind.

Rise and put on your running gear

and tweak your ankle walking
down the front steps

cry through your daily exercise

and grind.

Rise

and see Donald Trump primed to
become the standard bearer of a
major American political party

listen to The Doors' "The End"

and grind.

Rise with the
understanding

that honest, hard work pays off

know with soul-crushing certainty
that this is not true

and grind.

Rise next to a person
who loves you

with another, smaller person down
the hall who loves you

question your slightest
discontentment

and grind.

Rise

to attend a funeral

then work all day doing something
you hate

thinking of something you love

ignore the dissonance and grind.

Rise, hustling out the door

and place your coffee on your car roof

watch it fly down the highway

and grind.

Rise, trapped in the past

knowing the past is dead

and that you're living in death

try not to be a zombie and grind.

Rise

with your kid vomiting everywhere

knowing you'll upchuck soon
enough

and grind.

Rise

so sick of being sick

questioning Western medicine's
obsession with symptoms rather
than causes

take your medicine and grind.

Rise behind the wall
you've built

brick by brick

like Pink, wondering if there's
somebody out there

and grind.

Rise

and wash and eat and drive and
walk and talk and smile and fake
and sit and stare and drive and
wash and close your eyes

and grind.

Rise

and side with your head over your
heart, time and again

like a good, upstanding citizen

dismiss that burning question and grind.

Rise with an ice pick in your head

hoping your liver still functions,
having tested its limits

and grind.

Rise

and sell little pieces of yourself for money

hoping you can buy them back every weekend

and grind.

Rise and refuse to grind

letting your alarm clock know how
you feel about being a slave to it

speed to work in a cold panic

and grind.

Rise with a momentary understanding

that time is a fiction

ruling everyone, everywhere

like an emperor with no clothes

watch cat videos on YouTube and grind.

Rise

and run, run, run, run, run, run,
run, run, run

worrying about the time you want
to save

and run

and grind.

Rise with the invisible hand of the market

slapping you in the face

understanding its unflinching
brutality is most effective

and grind.

Rise

refusing to be manipulated by
moving pictures

give up and let the tidal wave of
manipulation wash over you

and grind.

Rise

recalling a dream you had in which
you were rich and free

an impossible dream

that has been inserted into your
brain

and grind.

Rise

with the pressure of a dozen beers
behind your eyes

and pretend you regret nothing

and grind.

Rise

and thank God it's Friday

without considering that one day,
you'll thank God for any day

even a god forsaken Monday

and grind.

Rise and grind with
the best of them

> while the best of them don't know
> why they're grinding
>
> or for whom they're grinding

and grind.

Rise and settle in
behind that blank page

feel exhilarated, titillated, endowed
by something beyond you

watch YouTube videos
and grind.

Rise

and write a heartfelt apology letter
to your body

for the horrible things you put it
through last night

and grind.

Rise with stories of
unfathomable anguish
and death blaring from
the radio

gripe that your coffee's too cold
and the weather's too hot

and grind.

Rise

and fall down the stairs, head over
heels

try to convince your boss that
you're injured

hear the disbelief in her voice and grind.

Rise from a disturbed sleep

wondering if that demon
represented something

shaking at the memory of its breath
on your face

and grind.

Rise

dedicated to unyielding,
unflinching, unapologetic
positivity

but today is a bad hair day

so give up and grind.

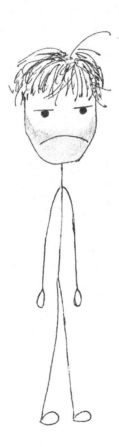

Rise with rust on your mind

the rust that never sleeps

squelch that part of you that wants
to burn out

before the rust has its way

and grind.

Rise

and make it

take it

fake it

until you return to that sanctuary,
free from making and taking and
faking

and grind.

Rise

and embrace the annual nightmare

the infernal office birthday party

smile through that mind-bending awkwardness and grind.

Rise and recall puppy love

and the scars of puppy love gone
wrong

or gone right, as it so happened

and grind.

Rise

to a text from your boss

who has a stomach bug

pray to every deity that he pukes
his guts out

and grind.

Rise

and cry in your office's utility closet

because it's sound proof

and you still have some semblance
of pride

and grind.

Rise

and sit through a morning meeting

with groaning and moaning and droning

ponder the dangers of a six-story fall

and grind.

Rise and go on with your bad self

because you're looking good today

damn good

pretend those jeans fit

and grind.

Rise

pay your car note, your mortgage
note, your student loan note and
your credit card note

note that you're suffocating

and grind.

Rise

and decide today is the day you'll
take up smoking

because Uncle Jeff's tracheotomy
didn't seem all that awful

and grind.

Rise

and get a haircut

one that makes you look like you're
ready to enlist

try not to puke

buy a hat and grind.

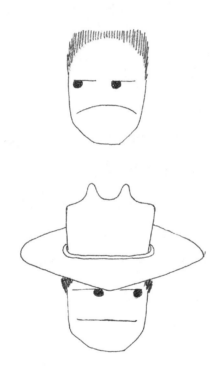

Rise and wonder
what's wrong with your
coworker's face

until you hear the tragic
background

hate yourself and
grind.

Rise on a rainy
Monday morning

and chastise the day for being a
harmful stereotype of Mondays

shake your head and
grind.

Rise

on a frigid January morning, sleet
coming down in buckets

and know nothing can be worse
than January

except February

and grind.

Rise on Valentine's Day

and let the series of chemical
reactions known as love do their
thing

and buy stuff for your lover

and grind.

Rise

with the echoes of the amplifiers
ringing in your head

from that god awful cover band

and grind.

Rise

and drink six seltzer waters before
noon

wonder if you have a problem

hear the bubbles call to you

and grind.

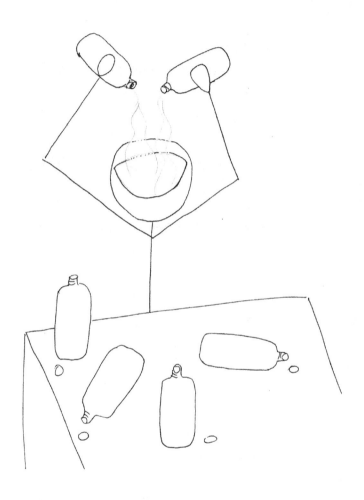

Rise

and hear people constantly referred
to as the GOAT

take your kid to the petting zoo

see the GOAT goat

and grind.

Rise

and push buttons, run water,
open drawers, open boxes, open
containers, pour, close, push,
pull, sit

eat breakfast

and grind.

Rise and shave

accidentally murder your
unsuspecting sideburn

apologize to the other as you kill it
for symmetry's sake

and grind.

Rise

daydream about the oligarchs
watching their gated communities
burn in righteous flames of justice

go to work and grind.

Rise with the memory of a good time

knowing you'll chase that good time

even though you apparently have a tattoo commemorating it

and grind.

Rise

aching from head to toe

after last night's co-rec softball
game

lie to your coworkers
about doing CrossFit
and grind.

Rise

and see that planet earth is blue

and there's nothing you can do

except to grind

and grind.

Rise

with screaming, crying, wailing,
teeth gnashing, pissing, puking
and defecation all around you

keep parenting and grind.

Rise

with a bubbleheaded, blow dried,
bellicose, bumbling bunch on the
news

scaring you between ads begging
for your cash

and grind.

Rise and check those
social media accounts

because oh buddy, that dopamine
feels so damn good

binge and grind.

Rise

and head to the voting booth

ignoring that nagging thought

that if voting made a fundamental
difference, it'd be outlawed

and grind.

Rise

with the news saying seltzer water
is bad for you

take up cliff diving, crocodile
hunting, smoking and
recreational drugs

and grind.

Rise

and read the news today, oh boy

that the only tried-and-true unity
is between psychopaths in the
Fortune 500

despair and grind.

Rise

and have an extra cup of coffee

stare at the ceiling 14 hours later,
unable to sleep

swear off coffee forever and grind.

Rise

with a thick layer of ice coating
your front steps

use $14 sea salt to melt the ice

and grind.

Rise

turn on the news

and watch Ayn Rand's most
fantastical fantasies unfold on the
screen

pray for the zombie
apocalypse and grind.

Rise

and accidentally swallow a swig of
your mouthwash

gag and grind.

Rise

and go to the gym

fall off the treadmill

happy that you now have an excuse
not to go to the gym

and grind.

Rise and dive into a Facebook flame war

fight and name call and rage and
rage and rage

until everyone loses

and grind.

Rise and have an
espresso

for a little pick-me-up

have a caffeine hallucination

shake and buzz and
grind.

Rise

and try to explain to the neighbor
why your kid told his dog to
delete its Twitter account

and grind.

Rise

after watching The Shining
before bed

tell your wife to remove the axe
from the shed, posthaste

and grind.

Rise

and contemplate how deflated
Jason Voorhees must've felt on
Friday the 12th

or Thursday the 13th, for that
matter

and grind.

Rise

and read that Nightmare on Elm Street was based on true events

purge that from your brain in a fit of Nope

and grind.

Rise

and go to a fancy beer spot after
work

refuse to admit that you enjoy lite
beer

suffer through the hops
and grind.

Rise

and tell a friend that the Internet is
the worst thing ever foisted upon
humanity

gripe about her reaction on Twitter

and grind.

Rise

and see that Facebook ads know
you better than you know yourself

and move to the wilderness

and cower in your cabin

and grind.

Rise and check your
credit score

because a man on his deathbed
regrets nothing like bad credit

worry and fret and
grind.

Rise and argue that George Orwell's darkest musings have come to pass

realize that pernicious things aren't easily labeled

and grind.

Rise

with shorter eyelashes than you
had before yesterday's cookout

because lighter fluid works quickly

wear sunglasses and grind.

Rise

and rise and rise and rise and rise

and grind and grind and grind and grind

until you're in a box, underground

and grind.

Rise

and have a practice shower cry

because today is Sunday

and fantasy football decisions await

so fret and grind.

AAAAAGGGHHHHH

Rise

and see that trumpeting love over
hate is merely strategic

since you can't out-hate a hater

love practically and grind.

Rise

with the wind at your back

and a gas bubble in your belly

blame your kid for the stench and grind.

Rise

intimidated to order at the posh
coffee shop

try to ask for a regular coffee

get something fancy and disgusting

drink it and grind.

Rise

with something crawling across
your foot

because camping is a special kind
of hell

make eye contact with
a bird-sized insect and
grind.

Rise

and watch a YouTube tutorial on
how to tie a tie

try and try and try until you want
to choke yourself with said tie

and grind.

Rise

and do nothing all day

and do nothing all night

stay up into the wee hours
lamenting what you didn't do

and grind.

Rise

and see that small birds could live
in the beard that has grown out of
your face

sprinkle birdseed in there just in
case

and grind.

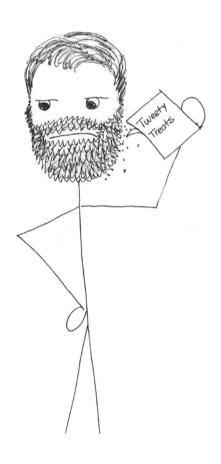

Rise and pick a side in
the class war

> think of yourself as a person of the
> people, for the people

keep trying to get rich
and grind.

Rise

and condemn lawmakers'
ambivalence toward mass shootings

while your kid plays with a toy gun

just call it a laser shooter and grind.

Rise

and love, love, love, love, love, love, love

because the clock never stops ticking

so take a break from grinding and love

and grind.

Rise

and shine

shine on

and if you can help it

don't grind.

Printed in the United States
By Bookmasters